BOOK BY KRISHNA KAPOOR

A Developer's Guide
STM TO IAR
MIGRATION

"STEP-BY-STEP INSTRUCTIONS FOR SEAMLESS CODE MIGRATION AND OPTIMIZATION"

A Developer's Guide
STM TO IAR MIGRATION

BOOK BY KRISHNA KAPOOR

CONTENT

1. **Introduction**
   - Overview of STM32 and IAR Workbench
   - Why migrate to IAR Workbench?
   - Who this guide is for
2. **Understanding STM32 and IAR Workbench**
   - Basics of STM32 microcontrollers
   - Introduction to IAR Embedded Workbench
   - Differences between STM32CubeIDE and IAR Workbench
3. **Preparing for Migration**
   - Assessing project compatibility
   - Tools and software prerequisites
   - IAR Embedded Workbench installation
   - STM32CubeMX and STM32CubeIDE setup
   - Backing up your STM32 project
4. **Setting Up the IAR Environment**
   - Configuring IAR Workbench for STM32
   - Installing STM32 support packages in IAR
   - Understanding the IAR Workbench project structure
5. **Converting STM Code to IAR Workbench**
   - Importing STM32CubeIDE projects into IAR
   - Handling differences in project files and folder structures
   - Updating compiler and linker settings
   - Migrating peripheral configurations (HAL/LL Drivers)
6. **Debugging in IAR Workbench**
   - Setting up the debugger
   - Connecting to STM32 target hardware
   - Using the IAR C-SPY Debugger
   - Common debugging issues and solutions
7. **Optimizing for IAR Workbench**
   - Configuring optimization levels
   - Analyzing and improving code performance
   - Using IAR's runtime analysis tools

CONTENT

8. Testing and Verification
- Running tests in IAR Workbench
- Validating firmware behavior on STM32 hardware

9. Troubleshooting Migration Issues
- Resolving compilation and linker errors
- Common pitfalls and their solutions
- FAQs for STM to IAR migration

10. Advanced Tips and Best Practices
- Leveraging IAR's advanced features
- Tips for maintaining cross-IDE compatibility
- Best practices for future development

11. Case Study: A Practical Migration Example
- Step-by-step migration of a sample STM32CubeIDE project
- Challenges faced and how to overcome them

12. Conclusion and Next Steps
- Recap of the migration process
- Exploring more advanced features in IAR Workbench
- Resources for further learning

Appendices
- A. STM32CubeIDE vs. IAR Workbench: Feature Comparison
- B. Useful Links and Resources
- C. Troubleshooting Reference

OVERVIEW OF STM32 AND IAR WORKBENCH

STM32 Microcontrollers

STM32 is a family of 32-bit microcontrollers developed by STMicroelectronics. These microcontrollers are based on the ARM Cortex-M architecture, offering a wide range of features and performance levels to suit various embedded applications.

Key highlights of STM32 microcontrollers include:
- Flexibility: Available in multiple series like STM32F, STM32L, and STM32H, catering to different power, performance, and application needs.
- Extensive Peripherals: Support for timers, ADC/DAC, communication protocols (UART, SPI, I2C, CAN), and more.
- Ecosystem Support: Compatible with development tools such as STM32CubeMX, STM32CubeIDE, and a wide range of third-party IDEs, including IAR Workbench.

These microcontrollers are widely used in industries like consumer electronics, automotive, healthcare, and IoT for their balance of performance, power efficiency, and cost-effectiveness.

IAR Embedded Workbench

IAR Embedded Workbench is a highly optimized Integrated Development Environment (IDE) tailored for embedded systems. It is renowned for its robust compiler, advanced debugging capabilities, and comprehensive analysis tools, making it a popular choice among professional developers working on STM32 and other microcontrollers.

Key features of IAR Embedded Workbench include:
- Highly Optimized Compiler: Generates efficient, high-performance code with advanced optimization techniques.
- C-SPY Debugger: Offers real-time debugging capabilities with detailed insights into code execution, memory usage, and peripheral states.
- Wide Microcontroller Support: Includes extensive libraries and tools for STM32 and other ARM-based microcontrollers.
- Static Code Analysis Tools: Helps improve code quality by detecting potential bugs and performance bottlenecks.

Why Migrate to IAR Workbench?

While STM32CubeIDE is a free and versatile platform, IAR Workbench is often preferred for:
Code Efficiency: Its compiler optimizations result in smaller and faster code, which is crucial for resource-constrained embedded systems.
Advanced Debugging: The C-SPY debugger provides detailed real-time insights that enhance the debugging process.
Professional Use Cases: IAR is widely adopted in safety-critical industries (automotive, aerospace, medical) due to its robust toolchain and compliance with industry standards.
Certification Support: IAR's tools are certified for use in applications requiring strict compliance, such as ISO 26262 for automotive safety.
By combining STM32's versatile hardware with IAR Workbench's powerful software tools, developers can achieve higher performance, reliability, and maintainability in their projects.

UNDERSTANDING STM32 AND IAR WORKBENCH

Basics of STM32 Microcontrollers

STM32 microcontrollers, developed by STMicroelectronics, are 32-bit microcontrollers based on the ARM Cortex-M architecture. Known for their versatility and scalability, they are widely used in a variety of applications, from simple IoT devices to complex industrial systems.

Key Features of STM32 Microcontrollers
ARM Cortex-M Core

STM32 microcontrollers use ARM Cortex-M cores, which offer a balance between performance and power efficiency. The different cores, such as Cortex-M0, M3, M4, and M7, cater to specific use cases:
- Cortex-M0/M0+: Ultra-low power, suitable for energy-sensitive applications like wearables.
- Cortex-M3/M4: General-purpose with enhanced performance and optional DSP instructions.
- Cortex-M7: High-performance core for advanced applications like image processing and control systems.

Wide Range of Peripherals

STM32 MCUs include a rich set of peripherals for diverse functionality:
- Communication interfaces: UART, SPI, I2C, CAN, USB, and Ethernet.
- Analog components: ADC, DAC, and Operational Amplifiers.
- Timers: Basic, advanced, and general-purpose timers for PWM generation, timekeeping, etc.

Scalability and Flexibility

STM32 offers a broad range of series tailored for different applications:
- STM32F Series: General-purpose, balancing performance and features.
- STM32L Series: Low-power series for energy-sensitive designs.
- STM32H Series: High-performance MCUs for advanced computing tasks.
- STM32G Series: General-purpose with enhanced efficiency and new features.
- STM32WB and STM32WL Series: Wireless connectivity for IoT applications.

Memory Options

STM32 microcontrollers offer flexible memory configurations, including:
- Flash Memory: On-chip memory for storing firmware.
- SRAM: On-chip volatile memory for runtime data storage.
- External Memory Interfaces: Support for external flash, SRAM, or SD cards for extended storage.

Low Power Modes

STM32 microcontrollers feature advanced power management modes, such as Stop, Sleep, and Standby, making them ideal for battery-powered devices.

UNDERSTANDING STM32 AND IAR WORKBENCH

Rich Ecosystem Support
The STM32 ecosystem includes tools like:
- STM32CubeMX: A graphical tool for configuring peripherals and generating initialization code.
- STM32CubeIDE: A free IDE with debugging and development support.
- HAL and LL Drivers: Abstraction layers for rapid application development.

Common Applications of STM32 Microcontrollers
Thanks to their diverse features and scalability, STM32 microcontrollers are widely used in:
- IoT Devices: Smart home systems, sensors, and connected devices.
- Consumer Electronics: Keyboards, audio devices, and wearables.
- Industrial Automation: Motor control, PLCs, and factory automation.
- Medical Equipment: Portable diagnostics and monitoring devices.
- Automotive: Infotainment systems and safety-critical applications.

STM32 microcontrollers provide a robust foundation for embedded system designs. Their combination of performance, power efficiency, and extensive peripheral support makes them a top choice for developers in various domains.

UNDERSTANDING STM32 AND IAR WORKBENCH

Introduction to IAR Embedded Workbench
IAR Embedded Workbench is a complete development environment designed specifically for embedded systems. Developed by IAR Systems, it is widely recognized for its powerful compiler, advanced debugging tools, and comprehensive support for a variety of microcontrollers, including STM32. It provides all the necessary tools for developing, debugging, and optimizing embedded applications in a single, user-friendly interface

Key Features of IAR Embedded Workbench

1. **Highly Optimized Compiler**
   - IAR's compiler generates efficient and compact code, ensuring optimal performance and memory utilization.
   - Advanced optimization techniques allow developers to balance speed and code size, which is crucial for resource-constrained embedded systems.

2. **C-SPY Debugger**
   - The C-SPY debugger offers real-time debugging with features like breakpoints, watchpoints, and peripheral registers monitoring.
   - It provides detailed insights into the microcontroller's runtime behavior, helping developers identify and resolve issues quickly.

3. **Comprehensive Microcontroller Support**
   - IAR Embedded Workbench supports a wide range of microcontroller families, including the STM32 series.
   - Includes pre-configured startup files, linker scripts, and device drivers for quick setup and development.

4. **Static and Runtime Analysis Tools**
   - Integrated tools like the Code Analysis and Runtime Analysis modules help improve code quality and system performance.
   - Detect potential bugs, memory leaks, and performance bottlenecks during development.

5. **Cross-Platform Debugging**
   - IAR Workbench supports debugging on real hardware and simulators, providing flexibility in testing and development workflows.

6. **Certification Support**
   - IAR is compliant with various industry standards like ISO 26262 (automotive) and IEC 61508 (functional safety), making it a preferred choice for safety-critical applications.

Why Choose IAR Embedded Workbench?
IAR Workbench is favored by professional developers due to its emphasis on efficiency, reliability, and scalability:

- Efficiency: Its optimized compiler ensures applications are fast and memory-efficient, critical for embedded systems.
- Ease of Use: The intuitive interface and extensive support documentation reduce the learning curve.
- Industry Adoption: Many industries, including automotive, aerospace, and medical, rely on IAR Workbench for its robust features and compliance with certification standards.

UNDERSTANDING STM32 AND IAR WORKBENCH

Why Choose IAR Embedded Workbench?
IAR Workbench is favored by professional developers due to its emphasis on efficiency, reliability, and scalability:
- Efficiency: Its optimized compiler ensures applications are fast and memory-efficient, critical for embedded systems.
- Ease of Use: The intuitive interface and extensive support documentation reduce the learning curve.
- Industry Adoption: Many industries, including automotive, aerospace, and medical, rely on IAR Workbench for its robust features and compliance with certification standards.

Applications of IAR Embedded Workbench
IAR Workbench is used in a variety of embedded system applications:
- Consumer Electronics: Efficient development for products like smart devices, wearables, and home automation systems.
- Industrial Systems: Developing motor controllers, industrial automation systems, and safety-critical solutions.
- Medical Devices: Ensuring compliance with strict safety and reliability standards in healthcare.
- Automotive Electronics: Supporting advanced driver-assistance systems (ADAS), infotainment, and other in-vehicle systems.

IAR Embedded Workbench provides developers with a robust platform to create, debug, and optimize embedded applications. Its rich feature set and industry compliance make it an essential tool for professional embedded development.

UNDERSTANDING STM32 AND IAR WORKBENCH

Differences Between STM32CubeIDE and IAR Workbench

STM32CubeIDE and IAR Embedded Workbench are both widely used for STM32 microcontroller development. However, they differ significantly in their features, target audience, and use cases. Below is a comparison:

	STM32CubeIDE	**IAR Workbench**
Purpose and Target Audience	<ul><li>Purpose: Open-source, integrated development environment (IDE) provided by STMicroelectronics for STM32 microcontrollers.</li><li>Target Audience: Beginners, hobbyists, and developers seeking a free and simple solution for STM32 projects.</li></ul>	<ul><li>Purpose: A commercial-grade IDE designed for optimizing performance, debugging, and certification in embedded systems.</li><li>Target Audience: Professional developers, especially those working on safety-critical or resource-constrained applications.</li></ul>
Licensing and Cost	STM32CubeIDE: Free to use.	IAR Workbench: Requires a paid license (options include trial, base, and functional safety packages). Its cost is justified by its advanced features and compliance certifications.
Compiler	<ul><li>Uses the **GNU Arm Embedded Toolchain** (gcc), an open-source compiler.</li><li>Focuses on general-purpose usage with moderate optimization capabilities.</li></ul>	<ul><li>Features the IAR C/C++ Compiler, known for generating highly optimized, compact, and fast code.</li><li>Ideal for resource-constrained environments, ensuring better memory and execution efficiency.</li></ul>

UNDERSTANDING STM32 AND IAR WORKBENCH

	STM32CubeIDE	IAR Workbench
Debugging Tools	<ul><li>Offers basic debugging features like breakpoints, variable watches, and peripheral register views.</li><li>Relies on open-source GDB (GNU Debugger).</li></ul>	<ul><li>Includes the C-SPY Debugger, which offers advanced debugging capabilities such as execution profiling, runtime stack analysis, and real-time data monitoring.</li><li>Supports trace debugging and performance analysis tools for in-depth troubleshooting.</li></ul>
Optimization	<ul><li>STM32CubeIDE: Basic optimization options for debugging and release builds.</li></ul>	<ul><li>Advanced optimization features tailored for speed, code size, or a balance of both.</li><li>Provides static and runtime analysis tools to improve performance and code quality.</li></ul>
Certification and Compliance	<ul><li>STM32CubeIDE: Does not have built-in features for compliance with industry safety standards</li></ul>	<ul><li>IAR Workbench: Offers compliance packages for standards like ISO 26262 (automotive) and IEC 61508 (functional safety), making it ideal for safety-critical applications.</li></ul>
Microcontroller Support	<ul><li>STM32CubeIDE: Exclusively supports STM32 microcontrollers with native integration of STM32CubeMX for peripheral configuration.</li></ul>	<ul><li>IAR Workbench: Supports a broader range of microcontrollers, including STM32, making it versatile for multi-platform projects.</li></ul>
Ease of Use	<ul><li>Easier to set up and use, especially for beginners.</li><li>Integration with STM32CubeMX simplifies peripheral initialization and code generation.</li></ul>	<ul><li>Has a steeper learning curve but provides better documentation and professional tools for advanced users.</li><li>Requires manual configuration for some STM32-specific features.</li></ul>

UNDERSTANDING STM32 AND IAR WORKBENCH

	STM32CubeIDE	**IAR Workbench**
Ecosystem Integration	• STM32CubeIDE: Seamlessly integrates with ST tools like STM32CubeMX and CubeProgrammer.	• IAR Workbench: Integrates with IAR's proprietary tools but also supports third-party tools and hardware.
Performance and Reliability	• STM32CubeIDE: Reliable for small to medium-scale projects with moderate optimization needs.	• IAR Workbench: Designed for high-performance, mission-critical applications where reliability and code efficiency are paramount.

When to Use Which?

Use STM32CubeIDE if:
You're a beginner or working on hobbyist projects.
You need a free, easy-to-use IDE for STM32 development.

Use IAR Workbench if:
You're a professional developer working on safety-critical or performance-sensitive applications.
You need advanced debugging, high code optimization, or compliance with industry standards.

PREPARING FOR MIGRATION

Certainly! Here's a detailed breakdown of each section for preparing to migrate an STM32 project from STM32CubeIDE to IAR Workbench:

1. Assessing Project Compatibility

Before migrating your STM32 project, it's essential to assess its compatibility with IAR Workbench. This ensures that the migration process will be smooth and minimizes potential issues.

Key Considerations:
- Hardware Configuration:
  - Review the microcontroller model and peripheral setup used in your STM32CubeIDE project. Ensure that the STM32 microcontroller you are using is supported by IAR Workbench.
  - Check if your project uses specific peripherals, such as timers, ADC, UART, SPI, etc. IAR Workbench supports a wide range of peripherals, but you should verify that your configuration can be easily transferred.
- HAL/LL Library Dependencies:
  - HAL (Hardware Abstraction Layer) and LL (Low Layer) libraries provide drivers for STM32 peripherals. Ensure that the HAL or LL libraries used in your STM32CubeIDE project are compatible with IAR Workbench.
  - If you've customized any HAL/LL code in your project, ensure that IAR Workbench can support these modifications, or prepare to refactor the code if needed.
- Middleware Compatibility:
  - Projects that utilize middleware, such as USB, TCP/IP stack, or FreeRTOS, need special attention. Ensure the middleware is compatible with IAR Workbench or can be integrated smoothly after migration.
  - For example, if you're using FreeRTOS, make sure the port used in STM32CubeIDE is compatible with IAR, or you may need to port it to IAR Workbench manually.
- Project Settings and Build Configuration:
  - Review build configurations like compiler settings, linker scripts, and startup files in STM32CubeIDE. These might need adjustments or reconfiguration in IAR Workbench.
  - Pay attention to optimization settings and warnings that may be set differently in IAR Workbench's compiler.

By evaluating these factors, you can identify any necessary changes or dependencies that need to be addressed before migrating the project to IAR Workbench.

PREPARING FOR MIGRATION

2. Tools and Software Prerequisites

To set up the development environment in IAR Workbench and ensure a smooth migration, you must install specific software tools and libraries. Here's what you'll need:

Required Tools:
- IAR Embedded Workbench for ARM:
    - This is the core IDE used for building and debugging STM32 projects in IAR. It includes the IAR C/C++ Compiler, C-SPY debugger, and a suite of optimization tools.
    - You can download it from the IAR Systems website. IAR offers various licenses, including a 30-day free trial for new users.
- STM32CubeMX:
    - STM32CubeMX is a tool provided by STMicroelectronics to configure the STM32 microcontroller's hardware features. It generates initialization code for peripherals, clock configurations, and system settings, making it easier to migrate from STM32CubeIDE to IAR Workbench.
    - It also helps in generating project files that can be imported into IAR Workbench.
- ST-Link/V2 or other Debugger Tools:
    - A hardware debugger such as ST-Link is necessary to connect your STM32 microcontroller to the PC. It allows you to debug, flash, and test the firmware on the hardware.
    - Ensure that your IAR Workbench installation is configured to communicate with the ST-Link hardware for debugging.
- Firmware and Device Libraries:
    - You will need the STM32 HAL or LL libraries (specific to your STM32 device) to facilitate peripheral management. These libraries are available from the STM32CubeMX or STMicroelectronics website.
    - Additional middleware (e.g., FreeRTOS, USB drivers) should be downloaded and checked for compatibility.
- IAR Add-ons:
    - IAR Workbench offers several add-ons (like IAR Systems' Run-time Environment, IAR Safety Packages, etc.) that are useful for advanced debugging and compliance features. Install any required add-ons based on your project needs.

PREPARING FOR MIGRATION

3. IAR Embedded Workbench Installation
Installing IAR Embedded Workbench is a critical step to setting up your migration environment. Here's how to do it:
Installation Steps:
- Download the Installer:
  - Go to the IAR Systems website and download the latest version of IAR Embedded Workbench for ARM. Make sure you download the version that supports STM32 microcontrollers.
- Run the Setup Wizard:
  - After downloading, run the installer. Follow the installation prompts to select the components you need. For STM32 development, ensure that the ARM toolchain and related components are selected.
- Activation:
  - IAR Workbench is a commercial product, so you'll need to activate it using a license key. If you are using a trial version, you can start by using the 30-day free trial license.
- Set Up Environment Variables:
  - After installation, ensure that the necessary environment variables (e.g., path to the compiler) are set correctly. IAR typically handles this automatically during installation, but it's good practice to double-check.
- Verify Installation:
  - Open IAR Workbench and check that everything is installed correctly by creating a simple STM32 project or using an example project to verify compilation and debugging capabilities.

4. STM32CubeMX and STM32CubeIDE Setup
If you're transitioning from STM32CubeIDE, you'll need to configure both STM32CubeMX and STM32CubeIDE to generate initialization code that can be used in IAR Workbench.
STM32CubeMX Setup:
- Generate Initialization Code:
  - Open STM32CubeMX, select the correct STM32 microcontroller or development board, and configure the peripherals, clocks, and middleware.
  - Generate the initialization code. In STM32CubeMX, choose IAR as the toolchain for code generation.
- Export Code:
  - Once the project is configured, export the generated code. STM32CubeMX can generate code compatible with IAR Workbench, including initialization code, HAL/LL libraries, and startup files.
- Check for Errors:
  - Review the generated code for errors or warnings that might affect the migration process. Ensure that there are no STM32CubeIDE-specific settings that need to be adjusted for IAR compatibility.

STM32CubeIDE Setup (if applicable):
- If your project was previously developed in STM32CubeIDE, ensure that all configurations are up-to-date. Then, export the relevant files (such as .ioc files or code files) for migration to IAR Workbench.

PREPARING FOR MIGRATION

5. Backing Up Your STM32 Project
Before proceeding with the migration, it's crucial to back up your entire project to avoid data loss. This step ensures you have a recovery option if anything goes wrong during migration.

Backup Strategy:
- Manual Backup:
  - Copy the entire project directory (source files, configuration files, libraries, and hardware abstraction layers) to an external or cloud storage.
- Version Control (Recommended):
  - Use a version control system like Git to manage your project. Commit your entire project to a Git repository so you can track changes and revert to previous versions if needed.
- Backup External Dependencies:
  - If your project relies on external libraries or middleware, ensure they are backed up or that you have access to their source code.
- Document Custom Configurations:
  - Document any special configurations or customizations you have made to the STM32CubeIDE project, as these might need to be re-applied after migration.

Conclusion of the Preparing for Migration Section
By completing these preparatory steps—assessing compatibility, setting up the necessary tools, installing IAR Workbench, configuring STM32CubeMX, and backing up your project—you'll be ready to begin migrating your STM32 project from STM32CubeIDE to IAR Workbench. The goal of this preparation phase is to minimize the risks and potential errors during migration, ensuring a smooth transition to a professional-grade development environment.

PREPARING FOR MIGRATION

5. Backing Up Your STM32 Project
Before proceeding with the migration, it's crucial to back up your entire project to avoid data loss. This step ensures you have a recovery option if anything goes wrong during migration.
Backup Strategy:
- Manual Backup:
    - Copy the entire project directory (source files, configuration files, libraries, and hardware abstraction layers) to an external or cloud storage.
- Version Control (Recommended):
    - Use a version control system like Git to manage your project. Commit your entire project to a Git repository so you can track changes and revert to previous versions if needed.
- Backup External Dependencies:
    - If your project relies on external libraries or middleware, ensure they are backed up or that you have access to their source code.
- Document Custom Configurations:
    - Document any special configurations or customizations you have made to the STM32CubeIDE project, as these might need to be re-applied after migration.

Conclusion of the Preparing for Migration Section
By completing these preparatory steps—assessing compatibility, setting up the necessary tools, installing IAR Workbench, configuring STM32CubeMX, and backing up your project—you'll be ready to begin migrating your STM32 project from STM32CubeIDE to IAR Workbench. The goal of this preparation phase is to minimize the risks and potential errors during migration, ensuring a smooth transition to a professional-grade development environment.

SETTING UP THE IAR ENVIRONMENT

Setting up the IAR environment for STM32 development is a critical step to ensure that your project will compile, debug, and run correctly. This section explains how to configure IAR Workbench for STM32, install necessary support packages, and understand the project structure.

1. Configuring IAR Workbench for STM32
Configuring IAR Workbench for STM32 development involves adjusting the IDE and compiler settings to ensure it works with STM32 microcontrollers.
Steps to Configure IAR Workbench:
- Create a New Project:
- After launching IAR Workbench, the first step is to create a new project. You can do this by selecting File > New > Project. From here, choose an Empty Project or select an appropriate template for STM32. If you want to use the STM32CubeMX-generated files, import the generated code into IAR Workbench.
- Select the STM32 Device:
- Once the project is created, you need to select the STM32 microcontroller that you are working with. Go to the Project options and choose the specific STM32 device or development board you are using. IAR Workbench supports various STM32 models and lets you specify the exact model for proper optimization and configuration.
- Set Compiler and Linker Options:
- IAR Workbench uses the IAR C/C++ Compiler for building projects. You need to adjust the compiler and linker options to ensure they are tailored to your STM32 project:
    - Optimization Settings: Choose the level of optimization you need (Speed, Size, or Balanced). STM32 projects often require careful optimization to reduce memory usage and improve execution speed.
    - Include Paths: In the Project Options, ensure that all paths to header files and libraries (like HAL/LL libraries) are correctly set. This allows IAR Workbench to locate necessary files during compilation.
    - Preprocessor Definitions: Make sure to add any required preprocessor definitions (like STM32F4xx for STM32F4 series) so that the correct STM32 headers and settings are used.
- Set Up Debugging Tools:
- To debug STM32 projects, you need to configure the debugging tool (like ST-Link) in Project > Options > Debugger. Select ST-Link (or another hardware debugger) as the interface. You can also configure debugging options like breakpoints, watchpoints, and the amount of data to be logged during debugging.

SETTING UP THE IAR ENVIRONMENT

2. Installing STM32 Support Packages in IAR

For IAR Workbench to work properly with STM32 microcontrollers, you need to install the appropriate support packages. These packages provide essential libraries, drivers, and configuration files.

Steps to Install STM32 Support Packages:
- Install IAR Embedded Workbench for ARM:
- When you install IAR Workbench, the base installation does not come with STM32 support by default. To add STM32 support:
    - Open IAR Workbench and navigate to Tools > Install additional components.
    - Select the ARM toolchain and STM32 support (if not already included in the initial installation).
    - This will include the STM32 libraries, linker scripts, startup files, and example projects required for STM32 development.
- Download STM32 Firmware Libraries:
    - HAL (Hardware Abstraction Layer) and LL (Low Layer) libraries are essential for interacting with the STM32 hardware. You can download them from the STM32CubeMX tool, which generates the initialization code, or from the STMicroelectronics website.
    - Once downloaded, ensure that the correct HAL/LL library version is added to your project folder, and configure the include paths in IAR Workbench.
- STM32CubeMX Integration:
- If you've used STM32CubeMX to generate initialization code, you will need to import the generated code into your IAR project. STM32CubeMX provides project files for multiple toolchains, including IAR, which can be imported directly into IAR Workbench for STM32.
- Verify Support Package Installation:
- After installing the support packages, verify that STM32-specific settings (such as linker scripts, startup files, and header files) are correctly included in your project. You can check this by navigating to Project > Options > Library and ensuring that STM32-related libraries are listed.

SETTING UP THE IAR ENVIRONMENT

3. Understanding the IAR Workbench Project Structure

IAR Workbench uses a specific project structure that organizes all the files and configurations required to build an STM32 project. Understanding this structure helps you navigate the IDE and manage the project effectively.

Key Components of the IAR Project Structure:

- **Project File (.ewp):**

The project file is the core of your IAR Workbench project. It stores all the configuration information, such as file references, compiler settings, and build options. This file is the first thing you'll open to work on your project in IAR Workbench.

- **Source Files (e.g., .c, .cpp):**

These are the C/C++ source code files that define the logic of your STM32 application. Typically, these include:
   - Main Application Code: This includes the **main.c** file, which contains the entry point of your application.
   - Driver Code: Code for interacting with STM32 peripherals using the HAL or LL libraries.
   - Interrupt Handlers: Code for managing interrupts in the STM32 microcontroller.

- **Header Files (.h):**

These files define function prototypes, macros, and external declarations used in your source files. They typically include:
   - Peripheral Initialization: Header files that define the structure and initialization functions for peripherals like GPIO, ADC, timers, etc.
   - Custom Code: Any user-defined header files for functions or variables shared between source files.

- **Startup Files:**

The startup files contain the assembly code responsible for setting up the microcontroller and initializing the system before the **main()** function is executed. These files are specific to the STM32 microcontroller and may vary depending on the model you are using.
   - STM32 Startup Files: These are part of the STM32 support packages and are responsible for configuring the memory regions (such as flash, SRAM), vector tables, and interrupt handling.

- **Linker Script (.icf):**

The linker script defines how memory is organized in the STM32 microcontroller. It specifies where different sections of the program (like the **.text** code section, **.data** section, etc.) are located in the microcontroller's memory. The linker script ensures that the program is correctly placed in flash memory and other memory regions.

- **Libraries:**

Libraries like the STM32 HAL or LL libraries are essential for peripheral management. These libraries are linked into the project to provide functions for configuring and using STM32 peripherals (e.g., UART, SPI, ADC, etc.).
   - HAL/LL Libraries: These provide high-level or low-level functions for interacting with the hardware.

- **Debugging Files:**

The debugging setup in IAR Workbench is stored separately from the main project files. These files contain settings related to breakpoints, trace, and watch windows. They help in debugging and profiling your STM32 application.

- **Generated Code:**

If you used STM32CubeMX to generate initialization code, the generated files will be part of your project. These files include the system clock configuration, peripheral initializations, and any middleware configurations that STM32CubeMX generates for you.

CONVERTING STM CODE TO IAR WORKBENCH

Converting an STM32 project from STM32CubeIDE to IAR Embedded Workbench requires careful migration of project files, configurations, and dependencies. This section explains each step in detail.

1. Importing STM32CubeIDE Projects into IAR

STM32CubeIDE and IAR Workbench have different project formats. STM32CubeIDE uses Eclipse-based project files, while IAR Workbench uses its proprietary format. Importing the project requires extracting key components and integrating them into the IAR environment.

Steps for Importing:

1. **Export STM32CubeIDE Project:**
   - Open your project in STM32CubeIDE.
   - Use the File > Export option to export the source code and configuration files.
   - Make sure to include all necessary files, such as:
     - main.c (application code)
     - HAL/LL library files
     - Peripheral initialization files
     - System and startup files

2. **Create a New Project in IAR:**
   - Open IAR Workbench and create a new project for your STM32 microcontroller. Use File > New > Project and select an empty project or an STM32 template.
   - Set the microcontroller or development board as per your STM32CubeIDE project.

3. **Add Source Files:**
   - Copy all the relevant .c and .h files from the STM32CubeIDE project into the IAR project directory.
   - In IAR, add these files to the project by right-clicking on the project in the Workspace window and selecting Add Files.

4. **Include Generated Code:**
   - If you used STM32CubeMX to generate peripheral initialization code, ensure the Core and Drivers folders are included in your IAR project.
   - Verify that the main.c file and any middleware configurations are properly included.

CONVERTING STM CODE TO IAR WORKBENCH

2. Handling Differences in Project Files and Folder Structures
STM32CubeIDE and IAR Workbench organize files differently. Adapting to IAR's project structure is essential for successful migration.

Key Differences:
- **Folder Structure:**
    - STM32CubeIDE projects often have a **Core** folder for application files (e.g., **main.c**) and a **Drivers** folder for HAL/LL libraries and middleware.
    - IAR Workbench requires you to manually organize these files into its project structure, ensuring all dependencies are correctly referenced.
- **Project Configuration Files:**
    - STM32CubeIDE uses **.project** and **.cproject** files for project settings, while IAR uses **.ewp** (IAR Embedded Workbench Project) and **.ewd** (debugger settings). These configurations are not directly compatible, so you need to reconfigure settings manually in IAR.

Steps to Handle Folder and File Differences:
1. **Reorganize Files:**
    - Move files from STM32CubeIDE's **Core** and **Drivers** folders into appropriate categories within IAR's workspace. For example:
        - Application code (**main.c**) goes under Source Files.
        - Header files (**stm32f4xx_hal.h**, etc.) go under Header Files.
2. **Adjust Include Paths:**
    - In IAR, go to Project > Options > C/C++ Compiler > Preprocessor.
    - Add include paths for the STM32 libraries (e.g., **Drivers/STM32F4xx_HAL_Driver/Inc**).
3. **Check Missing Dependencies:**
    - Ensure that all middleware and HAL/LL files are present and correctly linked in the IAR project.

CONVERTING STM CODE TO IAR WORKBENCH

3. Updating Compiler and Linker Settings

STM32CubeIDE and IAR Workbench use different compilers and linkers. Migrating a project involves updating these settings to match IAR's requirements.

Steps to Update Compiler Settings:

1. **Set Preprocessor Defines:**
   - In IAR, go to Project > Options > C/C++ Compiler > Preprocessor and add any preprocessor macros defined in STM32CubeIDE (e.g., **STM32F407xx, USE_HAL_DRIVER**).

2. **Add Include Paths:**
   - Add paths to the STM32 HAL/LL header files, such as:
     - **Drivers/STM32F4xx_HAL_Driver/Inc**
     - **Drivers/CMSIS/Device/ST/STM32F4xx/Include**

3. **Adjust Optimization Levels:**
   - Set the optimization level in Project > Options > C/C++ Compiler > Optimizations. Choose between speed, size, or balanced optimization based on project requirements.

Steps to Update Linker Settings:

1. **Linker Script:**
   - STM32CubeIDE uses **.ld** linker scripts, while IAR uses **.icf** (IAR Configuration Files). You need to configure the IAR linker file to reflect the memory layout of your STM32 microcontroller.
   - Open Project > Options > Linker > Configuration File and select the correct **.icf** file for your STM32 device.

2. **Memory Regions:**

Define flash and RAM memory regions in the **.icf** file. For example:

```
define symbol __ICFEDIT_region_ROM_start__ = 0x08000000;
define symbol __ICFEDIT_region_ROM_end__   = 0x080FFFFF;
define symbol __ICFEDIT_region_RAM_start__ = 0x20000000;
define symbol __ICFEDIT_region_RAM_end__   = 0x2001FFFF;
```

3. **Library Settings:**
   - In Project > Options > Library Configuration, ensure that IAR's runtime libraries are set up correctly. Select either full or minimal library configurations depending on your project requirements.

CONVERTING STM CODE TO IAR WORKBENCH

4. Migrating Peripheral Configurations (HAL/LL Drivers)

Peripheral configurations in STM32CubeIDE rely on HAL/LL libraries, which are fully supported in IAR Workbench. Migrating these requires careful setup to ensure that all peripherals are initialized and function correctly.

Steps to Migrate Peripheral Configurations:

1. **Verify HAL/LL Files:**
   - Ensure that the HAL or LL driver files (stm32f4xx_hal_gpio.c, stm32f4xx_hal_uart.c, etc.) are included in the IAR project. These files are typically found in the Drivers/STM32F4xx_HAL_Driver/Src folder.

2. **Include Peripheral Header Files:**
   - Add the necessary peripheral header files in your source files, such as:

   ```
   #include "stm32f4xx_hal.h"
   #include "stm32f4xx_hal_gpio.h"
   ```

3. **Reconfigure Clock Settings:**
   - If you used STM32CubeMX to configure the system clock, verify that the generated system_stm32f4xx.c file is included in the IAR project.
   - Check that the clock initialization function (SystemClock_Config()) is called in main.c.

4. **Handle Interrupts:**
   - Verify that interrupt service routines (ISRs) are implemented in the correct format for IAR Workbench. For example:

   ```
   void TIM2_IRQHandler(void) {
   HAL_TIM_IRQHandler(&htim2);
   }
   ```

5. **Test Peripheral Functionality:**

- Test each peripheral (e.g., UART, SPI, ADC) individually to ensure the configurations have been correctly migrated.

DEBUGGING IN IAR WORKBENCH

Debugging is a crucial part of embedded development, allowing developers to identify and fix issues within their code and hardware interactions. This section focuses on setting up the debugging environment in IAR Workbench, connecting to STM32 target hardware, leveraging the IAR C-SPY debugger, and resolving common debugging challenges.

1. Setting Up the Debugger
The IAR Workbench debugger integrates seamlessly with STM32 microcontrollers and offers advanced features such as breakpoints, watchpoints, and real-time variable tracking.

Steps to Set Up the Debugger:
1. **Select the Debugger Driver:**
   - Go to Project > Options > Debugger.
   - Choose the appropriate debugger driver, such as ST-LINK for STM32 microcontrollers.
2. **Configure Debugger Options:**
   - In the Debugger tab, configure the settings specific to your debugger. For example:
     - Driver: Select ST-LINK.
     - Interface: Choose between JTAG or SWD (Serial Wire Debug). SWD is commonly used for STM32.
3. **Set Download Options:**
   - In the Download tab, ensure the option to "Use flash loader(s)" is enabled. This ensures the code is correctly programmed into the STM32's flash memory.
4. **Enable Debug Information:**
   - Go to Project > Options > C/C++ Compiler > Debug Information and ensure debugging symbols are enabled for source-level debugging.

2. Connecting to STM32 Target Hardware
Establishing a physical connection between your STM32 microcontroller and the IAR Workbench debugging interface is vital for debugging real hardware.
Steps to Connect:
1. **Connect Debugger Hardware:**
   - Use an ST-LINK programmer/debugger or similar tool.
   - Connect the programmer to your STM32 board using either:
     - JTAG Interface: For full debugging capabilities.
     - SWD Interface: For a simpler, two-wire connection.
2. **Power the Target Device:**
   - Ensure the STM32 microcontroller is powered. Check the board's power supply and verify the connections.
3. **Verify Connections:**
   - In IAR Workbench, click Project > Download and Debug. If the connection is successful, the debugger will initialize and establish communication with the target hardware.
4. **Resolve Connection Errors:**
   - If the debugger fails to connect:
     - Verify the SWD/JTAG wiring and pin assignments.
     - Check the debugger interface settings in IAR Workbench.
     - Ensure the correct STM32 microcontroller is selected in the project options.

DEBUGGING IN IAR WORKBENCH

3. Using the IAR C-SPY Debugger

The IAR C-SPY debugger is a powerful tool for debugging applications running on STM32 microcontrollers. It provides a graphical interface to monitor and control the program execution.

Key Features of C-SPY Debugger:
1. **Breakpoints and Watchpoints:**
   - Set breakpoints to pause execution at specific lines of code.
   - Add watchpoints to monitor variable changes during execution.
2. **How to Set a Breakpoint:**
   - Right-click on a line of code in the editor and select Toggle Breakpoint.
   - Alternatively, use the Breakpoints Window to manage all breakpoints.
3. **Step Execution:**
   - Use the toolbar buttons to:
     - Step Over: Execute the next line without entering functions.
     - Step Into: Enter and debug functions.
     - Step Out: Exit the current function and return to the caller.
4. **Variable and Memory Inspection:**
   - Open the Watch or Locals window to monitor variable values in real time.
   - Use the Memory View to inspect and modify specific memory addresses.
5. **Real-Time Updates:**
   - Enable the Live Watch feature to track variable changes without halting execution.
6. **Call Stack and Execution Flow:**
   - Use the Call Stack Window to understand the sequence of function calls leading to the current state.
   - This is particularly useful for debugging crashes or unexpected behavior.

DEBUGGING IN IAR WORKBENCH

4. Common Debugging Issues and Solutions

While debugging STM32 projects in IAR Workbench, developers may encounter common issues. Here's how to address them:

1. Debugger Connection Fails:

Symptoms:
- Error messages like "Cannot connect to the target."

Solutions:
- Check the SWD/JTAG connections and wiring.
- Verify that the correct debugger interface is selected in IAR Workbench.
- Reset the STM32 microcontroller and try reconnecting.
- Update the ST-LINK firmware using the ST-LINK Utility tool.

2. Program Does Not Start:

Symptoms:
- The program doesn't execute after downloading.

Solutions:
- Verify that the correct reset vector is configured in the startup file.
- Check if the SystemInit() function in system_stm32xxxx.c is called before main().
- Confirm the correct clock settings in SystemClock_Config().

3. Debugger Doesn't Halt at Breakpoints:

Symptoms:
- Breakpoints are ignored during execution.

Solutions:
- Ensure the code matches the loaded binary (no compilation mismatches).
- Confirm that breakpoints are set in valid executable code.
- Check the optimization settings in Project > Options > C/C++ Compiler > Optimizations. High optimization levels can affect breakpoint accuracy.

4. Unexpected Peripheral Behavior:

Symptoms:
- Peripherals don't initialize or work as expected during debugging.

Solutions:
- Verify the initialization code for the peripherals.
- Check the clock configuration to ensure peripherals are correctly clocked.
- Inspect hardware connections for the peripheral.

OPTIMIZING FOR IAR WORKBENCH

Optimization in IAR Embedded Workbench focuses on improving code performance, reducing memory usage, and ensuring efficient execution on STM32 microcontrollers. This section details how to configure optimization levels, analyze and improve code performance, and leverage IAR's runtime analysis tools for achieving optimal results.

1. Configuring Optimization Levels

IAR Workbench provides a range of optimization settings that balance between code size, execution speed, and debugging capabilities. Proper configuration of these levels can significantly enhance the performance of your application.

Optimization Levels in IAR Workbench:

1. **None:**
   - No optimization is performed.
   - Best for debugging because the code closely matches the source.
2. **Low (Size):**
   - Prioritizes reducing code size without heavily impacting execution speed.
   - Useful for memory-constrained systems.
3. **Medium:**
   - Balances code size and execution speed optimizations.
   - Suitable for most embedded applications.
4. **High (Speed):**
   - Prioritizes execution speed, often at the cost of increased code size.
   - Ideal for performance-critical applications.
5. **Balanced:**
   - Offers a compromise between size and speed optimizations.
   - Useful for mixed-use cases.
6. **Maximize for Speed/Size:**
   - Maximum optimization is applied for either execution speed or code size.
   - Can make debugging more difficult due to extensive transformations of the source code.

How to Configure Optimization Levels:

1. Go to Project > Options > C/C++ Compiler > Optimizations.
2. Select the desired optimization level from the dropdown menu.
3. Adjust additional optimization settings, such as loop unrolling or inline function expansions, if needed.
4. For debugging, ensure that "Debug Information" is enabled to allow better traceability even with optimization.

OPTIMIZING FOR IAR WORKBENCH

2. Analyzing and Improving Code Performance

Optimizing performance requires a deep understanding of how the code interacts with the STM32 hardware and identifying bottlenecks in execution.
Steps to Analyze Code Performance:

- **Profiling Code Execution:**
    - Use the C-SPY Profiler in IAR Workbench to monitor execution times for functions.
    - Identify functions that consume the most CPU time or are called frequently.
- **Identifying Bottlenecks:**
    - Focus on functions or loops where execution time is disproportionately high.
    - Check for inefficient algorithms, unnecessary computations, or redundant function calls.
- **Improving Performance:**
    - Optimize Algorithms: Replace resource-intensive algorithms with more efficient ones (e.g., replacing nested loops with lookup tables).
    - Minimize Function Calls: Inline small functions to reduce overhead.
    - Use Efficient Data Types: Use the smallest data type that fulfills the requirement (e.g., uint8_t instead of int).
    - Leverage DMA: Offload data transfer tasks to STM32's Direct Memory Access (DMA) to free up CPU cycles.
    - Enable Compiler Intrinsics: Use compiler-specific intrinsics for tasks like bit manipulation or hardware-specific instructions.

Code Performance Metrics:

- Execution Time: Measure how long functions or sections of code take to execute.
- CPU Utilization: Determine how efficiently the CPU is utilized.
- Memory Access: Identify functions with excessive or inefficient memory access patterns.

3. Using IAR's Runtime Analysis Tools

IAR Embedded Workbench provides advanced runtime analysis tools that help developers monitor and improve application performance.

Key Runtime Analysis Tools in IAR:

- **Call Graph:**
    - Visualize function calls and their relationships.
    - Identify deeply nested calls or recursive functions that may impact performance.
- **Execution Tracing:**
    - Track the sequence of executed instructions in real-time.
    - Use this feature to debug and optimize critical execution paths.
- **Code Coverage Analysis:**
    - Determine which parts of the code are executed during testing.
    - Helps identify untested code paths or dead code that can be removed.
- **C-SPY Debugging Features:**
    - Cycle Counter: Monitor the number of clock cycles consumed by specific sections of code.
    - Event Log: Track and analyze runtime events such as function entry/exit, interrupt handling, and variable changes.

OPTIMIZING FOR IAR WORKBENCH

Steps to Use Runtime Tools:
- **Enable Runtime Analysis:**
    - Go to Project > Options > Debugger > Trace and enable trace functionality for your STM32 microcontroller.
    - Ensure that your target hardware supports trace debugging (e.g., using SWO or ETM).
- **Collect Runtime Data:**
    - Run the application in debug mode.
    - Use the Trace Window to view captured runtime data.
- **Analyze Data:**
    - Examine call graphs, execution times, and memory usage patterns.
    - Adjust code or configurations based on the insights.

TESTING AND VERIFICATION

Testing and verification are critical stages in embedded development to ensure the firmware meets the design requirements and functions as expected on STM32 hardware. This section details how to run tests within IAR Workbench, validate firmware behavior on the STM32 hardware, and ensure the final application is robust and reliable.

1. Running Tests in IAR Workbench
IAR Workbench provides a flexible environment for running unit tests, functional tests, and integration tests during the development process. These tests verify that individual components and the system as a whole operate as intended.

Types of Tests:
1. **Unit Testing:**
   - Focuses on testing individual functions or modules in isolation.
   - Ensures that each part of the code behaves as expected under various conditions.
2. **Integration Testing:**
   - Tests the interaction between different modules or components.
   - Verifies that data flow and communication between modules are correct.
3. **System Testing:**
   - Validates the behavior of the entire system, including all hardware and software components.

Steps to Run Tests in IAR Workbench:
1. **Set Up Test Environment:**
   - Define a testing framework within the project, such as Ceedling or CMock for unit testing.
   - Use custom test scripts or integrate third-party testing tools like Google Test.
2. **Write Test Cases:**
   - Create test functions for each module or feature.
   - Include edge cases, error conditions, and normal operation scenarios.

Example of a Simple Test Function:

```c
void test_Addition(void) {
    int result = add(2, 3);
    assert(result == 5);
}
```

3. **Compile with Test Instrumentation:**
   - Use the compiler options in IAR Workbench to include additional debug or trace code for testing purposes.
   - Enable coverage analysis to ensure thorough testing.
4. **Run Tests:**
   - Execute tests using the C-SPY Debugger or external hardware.
   - Monitor outputs in the Terminal I/O or Trace Output windows.
5. **Analyze Test Results:**
   - Verify test pass/fail status and review logs for failures.
   - Use IAR's Profiler or Code Coverage tools to measure test coverage.

TESTING AND VERIFICATION

2. Validating Firmware Behavior on STM32 Hardware

Validating firmware behavior involves deploying the application to the STM32 target hardware and performing real-world tests to ensure it functions correctly under actual operating conditions.

Steps to Validate Firmware Behavior:

1. **Flash the Firmware onto the STM32:**
   - Use IAR Workbench's Project > Download and Debug feature to program the firmware into the STM32's flash memory.
   - Ensure that the microcontroller is powered and connected correctly via ST-LINK or similar tools.

2. **Perform Functional Testing:**
   - Test individual features and peripherals, such as GPIO, UART, ADC, or timers, to ensure they behave as expected.
   - Use external instruments like oscilloscopes, logic analyzers, or multimeters to verify signal integrity and functionality.

3. **Example:**
   - If testing UART communication, send and receive data packets to verify baud rate, parity, and data accuracy.

4. **Stress Testing:**
   - Test the firmware under high loads or extreme conditions (e.g., high CPU usage, rapid I/O toggling).
   - This helps identify potential bottlenecks or failures in the system.

5. **Boundary and Edge Case Testing:**
   - Test the firmware's behavior under boundary conditions, such as minimum and maximum input values or unexpected inputs.
   - Verify the system's error-handling mechanisms, such as watchdog timers or fault recovery routines.

6. **Verify Timing and Performance:**
   - Use the Cycle Counter or Execution Time Analysis tools in IAR to measure function execution times and ensure timing requirements are met.
   - For real-time systems, confirm that interrupts and tasks execute within their deadlines.

7. **Hardware-In-The-Loop (HIL) Testing:**
   - Simulate real-world inputs and conditions using HIL setups to validate firmware behavior in a controlled environment.
   - For example, simulate sensor inputs and observe the system's outputs to verify correct operation.

Example Testing Scenarios:

1. **Blinking an LED:**
   - Use the STM32's GPIO to toggle an LED on/off and verify functionality with a multimeter or visually.
   - Test edge cases like invalid GPIO pin configurations.

2. **ADC Value Conversion:**
   - Connect an analog signal source to the STM32 and verify ADC conversion values against the expected results.
   - Use the IAR debugger to monitor register values in real time.

3. **UART Communication:**
   - Transmit and receive data through the UART peripheral and confirm data integrity using a terminal emulator (e.g., Tera Term or PuTTY).

TESTING AND VERIFICATION

Tips for Effective Validation:
1. **Log Results:**
    - Record test outcomes, including pass/fail status, error details, and timestamps.
    - Use tools like Excel or test management software to organize and track results.
2. **Automate Testing:**
    - Implement automated test scripts for repetitive tasks, such as running regression tests after every firmware update.
3. **Iterate Based on Feedback:**
    - Use the results from testing to refine and debug the firmware.
    - Address failures promptly and re-test until all test cases pass.

TROUBLESHOOTING MIGRATION ISSUES

Migrating a project from STM32CubeIDE to IAR Embedded Workbench can introduce challenges, such as compilation errors, linker issues, or unexpected behavior in the firmware. This section outlines how to resolve these issues, highlights common pitfalls, and provides a concise FAQ for typical migration-related questions.

1. Resolving Compilation and Linker Errors

During migration, differences in compiler behavior, settings, and project structures can lead to errors. Here's how to systematically address them:

Compilation Errors

These errors usually arise due to differences in compiler syntax, include paths, or unsupported directives.

1. **Missing Header Files:**
   - Problem: The IAR compiler cannot locate standard or custom header files.
   - Solution:
     - Check the Include Paths in Options > C/C++ Compiler > Preprocessor.
     - Ensure all relevant paths (e.g., STM32 HAL libraries, CMSIS, or application headers) are added.

2. **Unsupported Compiler-Specific Keywords:**
   - Problem: STM32CubeIDE uses GCC-specific keywords like __attribute__ or asm, which may not be compatible with the IAR compiler.
   - Solution:
     - Replace GCC-specific attributes with IAR equivalents. For example:
       - Replace __attribute__((aligned(4))) with #pragma data_alignment=4.
       - Replace inline assembly (asm) with __asm for IAR syntax.

3. **Data Type Conflicts:**
   - Problem: Differences in type definitions between STM32CubeIDE and IAR (e.g., uint8_t, int32_t).
   - Solution:
     - Ensure that stdint.h or CMSIS headers are included properly.
     - Avoid redefining standard types.

4. **Macro Expansion Issues:**
   - Problem: Macros used in STM32CubeIDE might behave differently in IAR.
   - Solution:
     - Use #define directives and inline comments carefully.
     - Verify macro expansions using the Preprocessor Output feature.

TROUBLESHOOTING MIGRATION ISSUES

Linker Errors
Linker issues often stem from incorrect memory layout, missing library files, or unresolved symbols.
- **Unresolved Symbols:**
    - Problem: Functions or variables are undefined during linking.
    - Solution:
        - Ensure all source files are added to the project.
        - Verify that startup files (e.g., **startup_stm32xxxx.s**) and HAL/LL drivers are included.
- **Memory Layout Issues:**
    - Problem: STM32 memory regions (e.g., flash, RAM) are incorrectly mapped.
    - Solution:
        - Update the Linker Script (or **.icf** file in IAR) to match the STM32 microcontroller's memory map.
        - Edit the **.icf** file in Project > Linker > Configurations to define memory regions correctly.
- **Library Compatibility:**
    - Problem: STM32CubeIDE libraries are incompatible with IAR.
    - Solution:
        - Replace GCC-compiled libraries with IAR-compatible versions.
        - Use IAR's CMSIS and HAL libraries provided in the STM32Cube firmware package.

2. Common Pitfalls and Their Solutions

1. Peripheral Initialization Issues:
- Problem: HAL/LL drivers don't initialize peripherals as expected.
- Solution:
    - Verify peripheral initialization settings in STM32CubeMX and ensure generated code is compatible with IAR.
    - Check for missing **#define** statements in **stm32xxxx_hal_conf.h**.

2. Interrupt Configuration Problems:
- Problem: Interrupts fail to trigger or behave unpredictably.
- Solution:
    - Ensure vector table settings in **startup_stm32xxxx.s** match the STM32CubeIDE configuration.
    - Verify NVIC settings and priorities in the **system_stm32xxxx.c** file.

3. Debugging Configuration Mismatch:
- Problem: The debugger fails to connect to the STM32 target.
- Solution:
    - Check the debugger interface settings in Project > Options > Debugger > Setup.
    - Match the interface (e.g., SWD or JTAG) and clock speed to the STM32 hardware.

4. Compiler Optimization Differences:
- Problem: Code optimized in IAR behaves differently from STM32CubeIDE.
- Solution:
    - Use the same optimization levels in IAR as in STM32CubeIDE.
    - Debug with optimizations disabled to isolate issues.

5. Clock Configuration Issues:
- Problem: Incorrect clock settings lead to peripheral malfunction.
- Solution:
    - Recheck clock configuration in STM32CubeMX and validate it in the generated code (**SystemClock_Config** function).

TROUBLESHOOTING MIGRATION ISSUES

3. FAQs for STM to IAR Migration

1. Why does the project structure differ between STM32CubeIDE and IAR?
STM32CubeIDE uses a flat file structure, while IAR Workbench organizes files into logical groups. Reorganize files in IAR to match its structure for better clarity.

2. How can I handle STM32Cube-generated makefiles in IAR?
IAR does not use makefiles. Instead, recreate the build settings (e.g., include paths, macros) manually or use the IAR plugin for STM32CubeMX to generate a compatible project.

3. Do I need to rewrite HAL/LL code for IAR?
No. HAL/LL libraries are compatible with IAR as long as their include paths and configurations are correctly set up.

4. How do I manage startup files during migration?
Replace GCC-specific startup files (e.g., startup_stm32xxxx.s) with IAR-compatible versions provided in the STM32Cube firmware package.

5. What should I do if debugging doesn't work after migration?
- Verify the debugger settings in IAR Workbench.
- Ensure the correct firmware is loaded onto the STM32 hardware.
- Check hardware connections and debugger compatibility.

ADVANCED TIPS AND BEST PRACTICES

This section focuses on advanced strategies and features in IAR Embedded Workbench to enhance productivity, ensure cross-IDE compatibility, and establish robust practices for future embedded development.

1. Leveraging IAR's Advanced Features
IAR Embedded Workbench offers a range of advanced features that improve debugging, code quality, and performance optimization.

1.1 Using the C-SPY Debugger Effectively
The C-SPY Debugger in IAR provides powerful debugging tools beyond basic breakpoints.
- Data Breakpoints: Monitor changes to specific variables or memory locations. For example, set a data breakpoint to detect when a variable exceeds a threshold.
- Trace Functionality: Capture and review execution history to analyze how the program reaches specific states.
- Real-Time Data: Observe variable changes in real-time while the program runs, without pausing execution.

1.2 Static Code Analysis with C-STAT
IAR's C-STAT tool helps ensure code quality and compliance with industry standards (e.g., MISRA).
- Benefit: Early detection of potential bugs, security vulnerabilities, and deviations from coding standards.
- Usage: Integrate C-STAT into your build process and review detailed reports to address issues proactively.

1.3 Runtime Analysis with C-RUN
C-RUN provides runtime error checking to detect issues such as:
- Buffer overflows, null pointer dereferences, and arithmetic overflows.
- Usage: Enable C-RUN in the Debug Options to track runtime errors during testing.

1.4 Power Debugging
For low-power applications, IAR offers power debugging tools.
- Benefit: Analyze the power consumption of your STM32 application.
- Usage: Use IAR's power probe (e.g., I-scope) to correlate code execution with power usage for optimization.

ADVANCED TIPS AND BEST PRACTICES

2. Tips for Maintaining Cross-IDE Compatibility
Maintaining compatibility between STM32CubeIDE, IAR Workbench, and other IDEs can future-proof your project and make it easier to migrate or collaborate.

2.1 Use Standardized CMSIS Libraries
CMSIS (Cortex Microcontroller Software Interface Standard) provides a universal abstraction layer.
- Why? It minimizes IDE-specific dependencies, making code easier to port.
- Tip: Stick to CMSIS-compliant peripheral access and avoid proprietary extensions unless necessary.

2.2 Modular Project Organization
Design projects with modularity in mind to simplify migration.
- Separate application logic, HAL/LL drivers, and startup code into independent folders.
- Use relative paths for include files instead of hardcoding absolute paths.

2.3 Avoid IDE-Specific Features
Refrain from using features that are exclusive to a specific IDE.
- Example: STM32CubeIDE's Makefile system isn't supported in IAR. Instead, rely on standalone scripts or tools for build automation.

2.4 Document IDE-Specific Settings
Keep a record of IDE-specific configurations, such as:
- Compiler options, linker settings, and debug configurations.
- This ensures smoother transitions if the project is moved to another IDE.

2.5 Use Version Control Systems (VCS)
Employ Git or another VCS to maintain a history of changes and make the project accessible across teams.
- Tip: Add .gitignore rules for IDE-specific files (e.g., .ewp, .ewd, .ewt) to avoid unnecessary clutter.

ADVANCED TIPS AND BEST PRACTICES

3. Best Practices for Future Development
Following best practices during development ensures project scalability, maintainability, and better performance.

3.1 Write Clean and Modular Code
Organize your code for readability and maintainability:
- Use descriptive variable and function names.
- Follow consistent formatting and naming conventions.
- Divide functionality into reusable modules.

3.2 Automate Testing and Validation
Incorporate automated tests for critical components:
- Use testing frameworks to automate unit and integration testing.
- Run regression tests after every update to ensure no functionality is broken.

3.3 Prioritize Debugging and Logging
Efficient debugging saves time during development.
- Integrate logging functionality into the firmware for runtime insights.
- Use conditional compilation (#ifdef DEBUG) to include/exclude debug-specific code.

3.4 Plan for Memory and Performance Constraints
Optimize code for the limited resources of embedded systems:
- Monitor stack and heap usage using IAR tools.
- Enable compiler optimizations (e.g., size vs. speed trade-offs).

3.5 Document Your Code and Configurations
Comprehensive documentation is invaluable for team collaboration and future reference:
- Include comments explaining key algorithms, peripheral configurations, and hardware setups.
- Maintain a README file with instructions for building, flashing, and debugging the project.

3.6 Stay Updated with IAR Tools
IAR regularly updates its tools and libraries to support new features and microcontroller families:
- Check for updates and incorporate them into your workflow.
- Join the IAR user community to stay informed about best practices and troubleshooting tips.

CASE STUDY: A PRACTICAL MIGRATION EXAMPLE

This case study walks through the complete migration of a sample STM32CubeIDE project to IAR Embedded Workbench. It includes step-by-step instructions, highlights the challenges encountered during the process, and provides practical solutions for overcoming them.

Step-by-Step Migration of a Sample STM32CubeIDE Project
For this example, we will migrate a basic STM32CubeIDE project that toggles an LED based on a button press using the STM32 HAL library.

Step 1: Preparing the STM32CubeIDE Project
1. **Generate the Project in STM32CubeIDE:**
   - Open STM32CubeMX and configure the microcontroller peripherals (e.g., GPIO for the LED and button).
   - Set up the clock configuration and initialize HAL drivers.
   - Generate the project with STM32CubeIDE as the selected toolchain.
2. **Verify the Project in STM32CubeIDE:**
   - Open the project in STM32CubeIDE and ensure it builds without errors.
   - Test it on the target hardware to confirm functionality.
3. **Backup the Original Project:**
   - Make a copy of the STM32CubeIDE project folder to avoid accidental loss or overwriting during migration.

Step 2: Preparing the IAR Embedded Workbench Environment
1. **Install STM32 Support Packages in IAR:**
   - Ensure the STM32 device family pack is installed in IAR via the Package Manager.
   - Verify that the required STM32 HAL/LL libraries are available.
2. **Set Up a New IAR Project:**
   - Open IAR Embedded Workbench and create a new project with the same STM32 microcontroller model.
   - Choose the correct startup file and linker script for the STM32 device.

Step 3: Importing STM32CubeIDE Project Files
1. **Copy Source Files:**
   - Copy application source files (main.c, peripheral configuration files) and include directories (e.g., Inc, Src) from STM32CubeIDE to the IAR project folder.
2. **Include HAL Libraries:**
   - Copy the STM32 HAL or LL driver files from the STM32CubeIDE project (Drivers/STM32xxxx_HAL_Driver) into the IAR project.
3. **Add Source Files to IAR:**
   - In the IAR project, manually add the copied source files and libraries to the project in their respective groups (e.g., Application, Drivers).
4. **Configure Include Paths:**
   - Go to Options > C/C++ Compiler > Preprocessor and add paths to all include directories (e.g., Inc, Drivers).

CASE STUDY: A PRACTICAL MIGRATION EXAMPLE

Step 4: Configuring Compiler and Linker Settings
- **Update Compiler Settings:**
    - Match STM32CubeIDE compiler settings (e.g., preprocessor macros, optimization levels) in IAR.
    - Define necessary macros like USE_HAL_DRIVER and STM32Fxxx in the compiler settings.
- **Configure the Linker Script:**
    - Replace the STM32CubeIDE linker script (.ld file) with the IAR-compatible .icf file.
    - Verify that the memory regions in the .icf file match the STM32 microcontroller's memory layout.
- **Set Entry Point:**
    - Ensure the project entry point (Reset_Handler) is correctly defined in the startup file and linker settings.

Step 5: Testing the Migrated Project
- **Build the Project in IAR:**
    - Compile the project and resolve any compilation or linker errors that arise.
- **Flash and Debug:**
    - Connect the STM32 hardware using an appropriate debugger (e.g., ST-Link).
    - Use IAR's C-SPY Debugger to flash the firmware and test its functionality.
- **Validate Peripheral Behavior:**
    - Confirm that the LED toggles as expected when the button is pressed.

Challenges Faced and How to Overcome Them
Challenge 1: Missing Include Paths or Files
- Problem: Errors like "file not found" or "undefined reference to HAL_Init."
- Solution:
    - Ensure all include paths from STM32CubeIDE are correctly added in IAR.
    - Verify that all required files (e.g., stm32fxxx_hal.c, system_stm32fxxx.c) are included.

Challenge 2: Compiler-Specific Issues
- Problem: GCC-specific attributes or syntax cause errors in IAR.
- Solution:
    - Replace GCC-specific attributes (e.g., __attribute__) with IAR equivalents.
    - Consult IAR documentation for compatible syntax or directives.

Challenge 3: Linker Configuration Errors
- Problem: Memory mapping errors, such as "region RAM is full."
- Solution:
    - Adjust the .icf file to match the STM32 device's memory regions.
    - Check for large global arrays or stacks exceeding available memory.

Challenge 4: Debugger Connection Issues
- Problem: The debugger fails to connect to the STM32 hardware.
- Solution:
    - Verify that the debugger interface (SWD or JTAG) matches the STM32 configuration.
    - Check hardware connections and ensure the correct driver is selected in IAR.

CONCLUSION AND NEXT STEPS

This final section recaps the key aspects of migrating an STM32CubeIDE project to IAR Embedded Workbench, introduces advanced IAR features to explore, and provides additional resources for continuous learning and development in embedded systems.

1. Recap of the Migration Process
The migration journey from STM32CubeIDE to IAR Embedded Workbench involves multiple structured steps aimed at ensuring a seamless transition while maintaining project functionality. Here's a summary of the key phases:

1. **Understanding Differences:** Recognizing the architectural and tooling differences between STM32CubeIDE and IAR, particularly in project structure, compiler/linker configurations, and debugging options.
2. **Preparing for Migration:**
   - Assessing project compatibility and gathering the required tools, libraries, and resources.
   - Ensuring a robust backup of the STM32CubeIDE project.
3. **Setting Up the IAR Environment:**
   - Installing STM32 support packages and configuring the environment for STM32 development.
   - Familiarizing yourself with IAR's project structure and options.
4. **Converting STM Code to IAR:**
   - Importing project files, adapting compiler settings, and resolving any mismatches in configuration.
   - Migrating peripheral initialization and driver code while ensuring compatibility.
5. **Debugging and Optimization:**
   - Utilizing the powerful debugging tools in IAR, including C-SPY and runtime analysis tools.
   - Fine-tuning the project for performance, memory usage, and power consumption.
6. **Testing and Verification:**
   - Running extensive tests in IAR and validating firmware behavior on STM32 hardware to ensure the migration's success.
7. **Troubleshooting and Advanced Techniques:**
   - Addressing common migration pitfalls, resolving errors, and implementing best practices for long-term maintainability.

CONCLUSION AND NEXT STEPS

2. Exploring More Advanced Features in IAR Workbench
Once comfortable with the basics of migration and IAR workflows, you can dive deeper into IAR's advanced capabilities to unlock its full potential:

2.1 Advanced Debugging
- Trace Debugging: Capture and analyze detailed execution flows to optimize time-critical code.
- Watchpoints: Monitor specific variables or memory addresses dynamically during debugging.
- Real-Time Data Monitoring: Observe changes in variables or system states without interrupting the program flow.

2.2 Code Quality Assurance
- Use C-STAT for static code analysis to ensure compliance with coding standards like MISRA and to detect potential vulnerabilities early.
- Employ C-RUN for runtime error checking to identify issues like null pointer dereferences or memory leaks during testing.

2.3 Power Optimization Tools
- Use IAR's power debugging features to correlate code execution with power usage, ideal for low-power embedded applications.

2.4 Multi-Core and Multi-Threaded Debugging
- For advanced STM32 devices with multiple cores or RTOS-based designs, IAR provides tailored debugging views to simplify complex workflows.

3. Resources for Further Learning
To enhance your skills and stay updated with the latest tools and techniques, leverage the following resources:

3.1 Official Documentation and Training
- IAR Embedded Workbench Manuals: Comprehensive guides for every tool and feature.
- STM32CubeMX Documentation: Reference for STM32 configurations and peripheral usage.
- IAR Academy: Offers online courses for beginners and advanced users.

3.2 Community and Forums
- IAR Developer Zone: Participate in discussions and get answers to specific questions.
- STM32 Community Forums: Engage with STM32 experts to troubleshoot challenges and share best practices.

3.3 Technical Blogs and Tutorials
- Explore blogs and tutorials focused on STM32 and IAR workflows for practical insights and real-world examples.

3.4 Open-Source and Sample Projects
- Study and experiment with open-source projects to gain hands-on experience in embedded development.
- Refer to STM32Cube firmware examples for practical use cases of HAL/LL drivers.

CONCLUSION AND NEXT STEPS

Next Steps

- **Experiment with Advanced Features:**
    - After completing a successful migration, experiment with IAR's tools for runtime analysis, power debugging, and static code analysis to improve your project's quality and efficiency.

- **Work on Larger and More Complex Projects:**
    - Use what you've learned to migrate and develop larger, real-world applications like RTOS-based systems or IoT projects.

- **Stay Updated:**
    - Keep an eye on updates to STM32Cube and IAR Workbench to stay compatible with the latest devices and tools.

- **Contribute to the Community:**
    - Share your migration experiences, custom scripts, or optimized configurations with the community to help others on a similar journey.

APPENDIX

A. STM32CubeIDE vs. IAR Workbench: Feature Comparison

This appendix offers a side-by-side comparison of STM32CubeIDE and IAR Embedded Workbench. It helps readers quickly understand the strengths, differences, and unique features of both IDEs. Key aspects covered include:

- Compiler Performance: GCC vs. IAR Compiler.
- Debugging Tools: C-SPY Debugger in IAR vs. STM32CubeIDE's debugger.
- Runtime Analysis: IAR's runtime tools vs. STM32CubeIDE capabilities.
- Supported Features: HAL/LL support, RTOS integration, and debugging options.
- Optimization Levels: Comparison of how each IDE handles code optimization.

This table helps developers decide when to use which IDE based on project requirements.

B. Useful Links and Resources

This section consolidates key resources to assist readers in learning more about STM32 development and IAR Embedded Workbench.

1. **IAR Embedded Workbench Resources:**
   - Official IAR documentation: Detailed guides for configuration and debugging.
   - IAR Academy: Online training courses for advanced features.
   - Technical support page: Troubleshooting and FAQs.
2. **STM32Cube Resources:**
   - STM32CubeMX user manual: Peripheral configuration guides.
   - STM32CubeIDE documentation: Debugging and project setup.
   - Firmware libraries: Links to HAL/LL drivers.
3. **Community and Forums:**
   - IAR Developer Zone and STM32 forums for expert discussions.
   - Embedded-related Stack Overflow tags for resolving common issues.
4. **Third-Party Tutorials:**
   - Blogs, YouTube videos, and GitHub repositories for practical insights and hands-on examples.

C. Troubleshooting Reference

This section provides a quick lookup table for resolving common migration issues encountered during the STM32CubeIDE to IAR Embedded Workbench transition. It includes:

1. **Compilation Errors:**
   - Missing headers or include paths.
   - Resolution: Ensure all source paths are included in the IAR settings.
2. **Linker Errors:**
   - Memory region conflicts in the linker script.
   - Resolution: Update the .icf file to match STM32 memory specifications.
3. **Peripheral Issues:**
   - HAL or LL initialization errors after migration.
   - Resolution: Verify the peripheral setup matches the STM32CubeMX-generated configurations.
4. **Debugger Failures:**
   - Debugger not connecting to the target hardware.
   - Resolution: Confirm SWD/JTAG settings and ensure the debugger driver is correctly installed.
5. **Runtime Bugs:**
   - Issues with code execution or unexpected behavior.
   - Resolution: Use IAR's runtime analysis tools to debug and analyze performance.

www.ingramcontent.com/pod-product-compliance
Lightning Source LLC
Chambersburg PA
CBHW040333220526
45473CB00009B/2666